HOW TO BE
THE MASTER
OF THE
STOCK MARKET

HOW TO BE
THE MASTER
OF THE
STOCK MARKET

Using the I Ching Stock Indicator to Decode the 64 Stock Price Patterns

MIKE NACH

HOW TO BE THE MASTER OF THE STOCK MARKET

TABLE OF CONTENTS

DISCLAIMER

The author and publisher have used their best efforts in preparing this book. The author and publisher make no representation or warranties with respect to the accuracy, applicability or completeness of the contents of this book. If you wish to apply the ideas contained in this book, you are taking full responsibility for your action.

Every effort has been made to accurately represent the techniques mentioned in this book and their potential. However, there is no guarantee that you will succeed in any way using the techniques and ideas in this book. Your level of success in attaining the results claimed in this book depends on your mental makeup/ belief system, knowledge and the time you devote to the ideas and techniques mentioned. Since these factors differ according to individuals, we cannot guarantee your success; in fact no guarantees are made that you will achieve any results from the techniques and ideas in this book. Nor are we responsible for any of your actions. Consulting a competent professional is advisable.

The author and publisher shall in no event be held liable to any party for any direct, indirect, punitive, special, incidental or other consequential damages arising directly or indirectly from any use of this material, which is provided "as is", and without warranties.

The author and publisher do not warrant the performance, effectiveness or accountability of any sites listed or linked to this book. All links are for information purposes only and are not warranted for content, accuracy or any other implied or explicit purpose.

U.S Government Required Disclaimer: Forex, Futures, Stocks and Options trading are not appropriate for everyone. There is a substantial risk of loss associated with trading these markets. Losses can and will occur. No system or methodology has ever been developed that can guarantee profits or ensure freedom from losses.

Hypothetical or simulated results have certain limitations unlike an actual performance record. Simulated results do not represent actual trading also. Since the trades have not been executed, the results may have under-or-over compensated for the impact, if any, of certain market factors, such as lack of liquidity or unforeseen circumstances.

THE I CHINGSTOCK INDICATOR

"If I have seen farther, it is by standing on the
shoulder of giants."
– Sir Isaac Newton

Wouldn't it be nice to have one indicator that does it all?

Duh?

I get it! Let me tell you about a hypothetical conversation which I had with my trader friend who I shall call Skeptic!

"Hey, Skeptic!" I yelled out, "Check out this new stock indicator developed by me."

"Are you kidding me?" Skeptic grimaced, "Aren't there enough stock indicators in the market? Is this some get rich quick scam?"

"Dow's sakes, Skeptic! Be positive," I retorted, "Check out what I have to say and then give your bloody comments."

"Go on. Tell me about it."

"Wouldn't it be nice to have an indicator that does it all?" I replied, "The I Ching Stock Indicator will give you the edge. This indicator is unlike any indicator developed in the past. It will tell you when to get in or stay out of the market. It will decode the hidden messages lurking within the stock price patterns. It's as if a market wizard is by

5

your side to hold your hand and show you the way in the treacherous jungle called the Stock Market."

"LOL!" Skeptic laughed out loud.

"Thanks," I continued, "The trouble with most technical indicators is that patterns, that allegedly predict the future, will already have been identified and acted upon by market participants following these systems. Each participant interprets the patterns as per his level of understanding."

"You bet." Skeptic nodded his head.

"Some market participants look at the past patterns of rising/ falling prices and assume that the market, in real time, will follow the same path. Déjà vu!" I continued, "Some traders will buy thinking the market will rise whilst other traders will consider the rising market as an over-bought situation and short sell the stocks."

"I agree totally," Skeptic interrupted, "Then, there's the situation where you have done your homework and taken a position. The very next moment, your chosen stock starts sliding downhill eroding your capital. It's so damn annoying. Markets are complex systems that are hard to analyze. Interpretation of technical indicators is more of an art than science."

"You nailed it," I said, "Market participants interpret the patterns in different ways and act accordingly. It is only when many of these participants see the same pattern and respond the same way, that the technical indicators become a wish fulfilling exercise."

"I get it. But, how's your indicator gonna solve the problem? And what's this I Ching stuff?" Skeptic asked.

"The I Ching is one of the oldest and uncannily accurate divination systems in the world. (Check out the next chapter.)" I answered, "It is a book of wisdom that makes **"Change"** the center of observation and identifies time as an important factor in the world's structure and human development. The stock market also depends on price changes with time. Based on the market participant's interpretation of the various situations affecting the listed companies, the stock prices keep on fluctuating during the entire trading period. The stock market discounts all available information and this is reflected in the stock prices. This may be true only for the information known at the time. But-

What if this information is not fully understood by the market participants?

What about information that is yet to originate (state of potentiality)?

The I Ching Stock Indicator comes into play here. There are 64 patterns or hexagrams in the I Ching system which you can use to interpret stock prices. You can use these patterns to decode the hidden messages lurking within these patterns. This is what you get if you use the I Ching Stock Indicator. The edge!"

"Wow!" Skeptic exclaimed, "I reckon I will check out your indicator. Will I be always right if I use your method?"

"Never be over confident when trading." I answered, "It is not possible to win 100 percent of the time even with the best trading method. What if you interpret the readings to fit your conviction? Our emotional state plays a great role in our success or failure in the stock market. The difference between great investors/ traders and the ordinary is their ability to remain calm and isolated irrespective of what the markets are doing."

Hey! Never force a trade and **don't use the I ChingStock Indicator as a standalone trading method to decide the trades for you.** Never base your trading decisions on any single trading indicator. If the I Ching Stock Indicator advises you to consult your broker or the price charts then please do so. A single day/ period's reading is not enough to decode a stock's future. Back testing the predictions for **prior periods** will give you a better picture of your stock."

"I am piqued," Skeptic spoke out excitedly, "Your indicator sounds promising. My skepticism is on hold. I will definitely try it out. Thanks!"

So, that's it, guys! Have faith and practice the timeless principles given in this book. Follow the advice of the I Ching Stock Indicator and you will be richly rewarded for your efforts.

Happy investing/ trading, Market Wizard!

ABOUT THE I CHING

The**I Ching, the Chinese Book of Change**, is an ancient and venerable book of divination. Its origins lie with Fu Hsi who ruled China before the flood (c. 3000 B.C.). The basic text was written by King Wen (1123 B.C.) and his son Duke Chou. The commentaries were written by Confucius (561-479 B.C.) and his followers.

It is one of the oldest divination systems in the world. It has been in existence for thousands of years and millions of people over the ages, from emperors to commoners, have used it and greatly benefited from its advice. You will, too. Consulting the I Ching is like having, by your side, a wise and all-knowing personality that is always ready to help and advice whenever you need it. The very fact, that it's still popular today means that it has something going for it.

The I Ching makes "Change" the center of observation and identifies time as an important factor in the world's structure and human development. The stock market also depends on price changes with time. Based on the market participant's perceptions of the information received by him/ her, the stock prices keep on fluctuating during the entire trading period. The stock market discounts all available information and this is reflected in the stock prices. This may be true only for the information known at the time.

The stock market is a place where the information is not always dependable. Often, there's no correlation between the company's performance and its stock price. Rumors and false information abound the market. A newbie participant can easily make huge losses in such a situation. This makes investing/trading a very scary operation. It is no wonder that most people stay away from the market!

You need to have an edge if you want to make money in the stock market. If you don't have an edge, all the discipline and money management skills in this world will be of no use. You will lose badly. **I am saying this again-** The I Ching Stock Indicator will give you the required edge. It will advise you when or what to invest/ trade or when to enter/ stay out of the market.

This book is designed for the beginner, intermediate and advanced investor/ trader. It will be your lifelong friend, prognosticator and guide.

Have faith and practice the timeless principles given in this book. Follow the trading advice given by the oracle and you will be richly rewarded for your efforts. If you are still in doubt, check the advice given against the actual market conditions. It is preferable that initially you paper trade so that you do not lose any money. Do back testing. After you become confident and proficient in this technique, start consulting the I Ching Stock Indicator during actual trading situations.

THE 64 PRICE ACTIONS CONFIGURATION

The Price Actions are configured as follows:

1. Let P be the price of a stock. It could be either the close price or the Pivot Point which is the average price (High+Low+Close divided by3) of the day. You can also use Japanese candlesticks to divine the stock market. Choose any one configuration. Once you decide this, stick with it.

2. Next we figure out the time interval between the prices. If you ask me, I would go with daily price changes. You could try out weekly, monthly or yearly periods and compare the accuracy for the various price intervals.

3. For creating our daily price action, we choose prices of seven consecutive days. If we need to figure out the future outcome for weekly intervals, we choose average prices of seven consecutive weeks. Likewise, if we need to know the monthly or yearly outcomes, choose the average monthly or yearly prices of seven consecutive months or years.

Does this make sense? Yes? Good!

4. Let P6 be the end(newest) or sixth price and P1 be the beginning (oldest) or start price; P2, P3, P4 and P5 will be the consecutive prices between the start and end prices. We will also need a price consecutively prior to P1, which we will name as P0, to determine the price action of P1.

13

5. If the price is greater than the price of the prior consecutive period we will call it a "+" price pattern.

If the price is less than the price of the prior consecutive period we will call it a "-" price pattern.

6. After you have figured out the + /- patterns, checkout the Action Lookup table and locate the Action No for your stock.

7. Read the predictions. Check out whether the advice makes sense and then take your investing decision accordingly.

ACTION LOOKUP TABLE

→ ↓	+ + +	- - +	- + -	+ - -	- - -	+ + -	+ - +	- + +
+ + +	1	34	5	26	11	9	14	43
- - +	25	51	3	27	24	42	21	17
- + -	6	40	29	4	7	59	64	47
+ - -	33	62	39	52	15	53	56	31
- - -	12	16	8	23	2	20	35	45
+ + -	44	32	48	18	46	57	50	28
+ - +	13	55	63	22	36	37	30	49
- + +	10	54	60	41	19	61	38	58

Find the upper half of your Action at the top (→) and the lower half on the left (↓) and follow the row and column to where they intersect. That will be the number of your Action.

Examples:

1. Close Price Method: Check out the stock prices for the period May 5, 2016 to May 13, 2016. Let us denote P0, P1, P2, P3, P4, P5 and P6 as the close prices of the stock on these dates.

Date	Open	High	Low	Close	Price	Action	
May 13, 2016	22.5	22.92	22.5	21.18	P6	P6>P5	✚
May 12, 2016	23.18	23.19	22.37	21.13	P5	P5<P4	▬
May 11, 2016	23.37	23.39	23.11	21.64	P4	P4<P3	▬
May 10, 2016	23.33	23.39	23.03	21.85	P3	P3>P2	✚
May 09, 2016	23.25	23.44	23.15	21.71	P2	P2>P1	✚
May 06, 2016	23.34	23.36	22.96	21.69	P1	P1<P0	▬
May 05, 2016	23.5	23.52	23.17	21.81	P0	Pattern 18	

As per the Action Lookup Table, the **stock pattern is 18**.

2. Pivot Point Method: Check out the stock prices for the period May19, 2016 to May 27, 2016. Let P0, P1, P2, P3, P4, P5 and P6 be the average daily (Pivot) prices (High+Low+Close divided by3) of the stock.

Date	Open	High	Low	Close	Pivot	Price	Action	
May 27, 2016	715	716.60	711.10	712.24	713.31	P6	P6>P5	✚
May 26, 2016	708.33	715.00	707.29	714.91	712.40	P5	P5>P4	✚
May 25, 2016	708	710.86	705.52	708.35	708.24	P4	P4>P3	✚
May 24, 2016	698.01	707.50	698	704.20	703.23	P3	P3>P2	✚
May 23, 2016	704.25	706.00	696.42	696.75	699.72	P2	P2<P1	▬
May 20, 2016	701.05	707.24	700	702.80	703.35	P1	P1>P0	✚
May 19, 2016	691.88	699.40	689.56	698.52	695.83	P0	Pattern 13	

As per the Action Lookup Table, the **stock pattern is 13**.

3. Open and Close / Japanese candlesticks method: I am not going to dive into Japanese candlesticks theory nor draw charts to illustrate this method. I am assuming you already know about candlesticks. If you need to know about candlesticks then there's lots of stuff about Japanese candlesticks in the internet. Please don't use this method with Heiken Ashi or other types of candle sticks. Just try the method with normal candlesticks.

Okay, Let's check out the six consecutive Open/ Close prices and their resulting candlesticks of a hypothetical stock starting with March 4 and ending with March 11, 2016.

Date	Open	Close	Candle	
11/03/2016	699.4	699.6	Green	+
10/03/2016	700.3	668.06	Red	-
09/03/2016	608.18	673.58	Green	+
06/03/2016	600.55	563	Red	-
05/03/2016	626.06	597.95	Red	-
04/03/2016	655.8	621.44	Red	-
			Pattern 35	

The candles of March 11 and 9 would be Green/ White which means the close prices were higher than the open prices on these days. Likewise, since the close prices were lower than the open prices, there would be Red/ Black candles on March 10, 6, 5 and 4. You will denote the Green/ White candles as "+" and Red/ Black candles as "-." Arrange the candles in the descending order of dates (as shown above) and checking out the Pattern Lookup Table, locate the pattern number, for the above configuration.

It is **pattern 35**.

ACTION 1: P6>P5>P4>P3>P2>P1>P0

Date	Price	Action	Pattern
End Date D6	P6	P6>P5	+
D5	P5	P5>P4	+
D4	P4	P4>P3	+
D3	P3	P3>P2	+
D2	P2	P2>P1	+
D1	P1	P1>P0	+
Start Date D0	P0		

The I Ching Says:

1.Have you figured out why the price of this stock has been consistently moving up the past six days?

2.Has the company's results beaten the analyst's estimates?

3.Is the market in an uptrend?

4.If you don't know the answers, why don't you ask the advice of your stock broker/ advisor before you trade this stock?

5. If you are hell-bent on investing in this stock then use stop loss to avoid a probable loss for this trade.

6.OR-Wait for a better opportunity or new information to present itself soon.

7. TIP: Have you checked out the competitors? Are any of these companies doing better fundamentally and technically? If yes, then why don't you invest inthese companies?

ACTION 2: P6<P5<P4<P3<P2<P1<P0

Date	Price	Action	Pattern
End Date D6	P6	P6<P5	-
D5	P5	P5<P4	-
D4	P4	P4<P3	-
D3	P3	P3<P2	-
D2	P2	P2<P1	-
D1	P1	P1<P0	-
Start Date D0	P0		

The I Ching Says:

1.Has the company's results fallen short of analyst's estimates? Check out the latest quarter results before you take the plunge.

2.This stock is exhibiting price volatility or selling pressure. Plan your entry/ exit points, stop loss before you trade.

3.After initial setback, the price of this stock will recover.

4.If it is a relatively unknown stock then it will soon become newsworthy.

5.Even if there is an upswing, later, market conditions are going to change which will adversely affect your stock. Buy on weakness and sell on strengths.

ACTION 3: P6<P5>P4<P3<P2<P1>P0

Date	Price	Action	Pattern
End Date D6	P6	P6<P5	-
D5	P5	P5>P4	+
D4	P4	P4<P3	-
D3	P3	P3<P2	-
D2	P2	P2<P1	-
D1	P1	P1>P0	+
Start Date D0	P0		

The I Ching Says:

1. If you need to buy this stock, limit your initial position in this stock. Increase position after watching its price action.

2.P6<P5.You will need to hold on to this stock for a while before the price moves up.

3.Wait for a better opportunity to present itself soon.

ACTION 4: P6>P5<P4<P3<P2>P1<P0

Date	Price	Action	Pattern
End Date D6	P6	P6>P5	+
D5	P5	P5<P4	-
D4	P4	P4<P3	-
D3	P3	P3<P2	-
D2	P2	P2>P1	+
D1	P1	P1<P0	-
Start Date D0	P0		

The I Ching Says:

1.There are two pluses and four minuses. Are there no better stocks at this price level?Don't invest/ trade in this stock if it has shown extreme price volatility in the past.

2.OR Invest/ trade in this stock only if the market is bullish and the company's fundamentals are good.

3.TIP: Your profit probabilities are higher with stocks of promising new companies.

ACTION 5: P6<P5>P4<P3>P2>P1>P0

Date	Price	Action	Pattern
End Date D6	P6	P6<P5	-
D5	P5	P5>P4	+
D4	P4	P4<P3	-
D3	P3	P3>P2	+
D2	P2	P2>P1	+
D1	P1	P1>P0	+
Start Date D0	P0		

The I Ching Says:

1.Wait. Don't invest/ trade in this stock now.Check out if there are lots of rumors and misinformation about this stock.

2.P6<P5- Wait for the price of your stock/ the market to stabilize before entering your position.

ACTION 6: P6>P5>P4>P3<P2>P1<P0

Date	Price	Action	Pattern
End Date D6	P6	P6>P5	+
D5	P5	P5>P4	+
D4	P4	P4>P3	+
D3	P3	P3<P2	-
D2	P2	P2>P1	+
D1	P1	P1<P0	-
Start Date D0	P0		

The I Ching Says:

1.The last three periods (P4, P5, and P6) are on the upswing. Is it sustainable? This stock could be a short term play.It will exhibit extreme price volatility. Exiting your position will be difficult.If you wish to jump in, plan your entry/exit points for this trade. Use stop loss.

2. Be patient.Don't invest/ trade in this stock now.Wait.After the volatile period subsides, the price of your stock will recover.

3.If you indulge in contrarian investing/ trading for this stock, you will lose.

ACTION 7: P6<P5<P4<P3<P2>P1<P0

Date	Price	Action	Pattern
End Date D6	P6	P6<P5	-
D5	P5	P5<P4	-
D4	P4	P4<P3	-
D3	P3	P3<P2	-
D2	P2	P2>P1	+
D1	P1	P1<P0	-
Start Date D0	P0		

The I Ching Says:

1.If your stock is of a poorly performing company, its price will be affected.There are five minuses and one plus. Expect a probable loss for this trade.Wait for present conditions/ trend to change before taking a position.

2. If you have decided this stock is for you, check out P7 and limit your initial position in this stock. Increase your position steadily only after its price action is clear (after P7).

3. TIP: Choose leading/ stable stocks,favored by insiders, institutions and analysts, especially if the market conditions are chaotic.

ACTION 8: P6<P5>P4<P 3<P2<P1<P0

Date	Price	Action	Pattern
End Date D6	P6	P6<P5	-
D5	P5	P5>P4	+
D4	P4	P4<P3	-
D3	P3	P3<P2	-
D2	P2	P2<P1	-
D1	P1	P1<P0	-
Start Date D0	P0		

The I Ching Says:

1.If your stock is of a recently downgraded companyor is an unknown, under-performing or thinly traded stock, don't take a position. The above pattern is showing weakness. Five minuses and one plus with P6<P5.

2. However, if your stock is showing a definitive trend, take a position.There is a high probability of unexpected profits from this trade at the right price. Short sell?

3.TIP: Investing/ trading in stocks of companies favored by analysts and institutional investors will be profitable.

ACTION 9: P6>P5>P4<P3>P2>P1>P0

Date	Price	Action	Pattern
End Date D6	P6	P6>P5	+
D5	P5	P5>P4	+
D4	P4	P4<P3	-
D3	P3	P3>P2	+
D2	P2	P2>P1	+
D1	P1	P1>P0	+
Start Date D0	P0		

The I Ching Says:

1.You will need to buy this stock on weakness and sell on strengths. Set up your buy/ sell targets. There could be a price reversal shortly.Be prepared for small profits.

2.The last six days have shown five pluses and one minus. Also, P5>P4 and P6>P5. If you are willing to accept a certain level of risk, then take a position.

3.TIP: Your profit probabilities are higher with leading stocks/ market favorites.

33

ACTION 10: P6>P5>P4>P3<P2>P1>P0

Date	Price	Action	Pattern
End Date D6	P6	P6>P5	+
D5	P5	P5>P4	+
D4	P4	P4>P3	+
D3	P3	P3<P2	-
D2	P2	P2>P1	+
D1	P1	P1>P0	+
Start Date D0	P0		

The I Ching Says:

1.Check out the price pattern for the earlier periods. Is there a discernible pattern? Are there more pluses than minuses? If yes, start small and then invest/ trade up in small lots. Plan your entry/exit points for this trade. Use stop loss. Stay with the trend/ pattern.

2. Wait. If you are a long term investor, don't invest in this stock now.

3. TIP: Trade in leading stocks of fundamentally strong companies for the long term.

ACTION 11: P6<P5<P4<P3>P2>P1>P0

Date	Price	Action	Pattern
End Date D6	P6	P6<P5	-
D5	P5	P5<P4	-
D4	P4	P4<P3	-
D3	P3	P3>P2	+
D2	P2	P2>P1	+
D1	P1	P1>P0	+
Start Date D0	P0		

The I Ching Says:

1.Three pluses and three minuses. P4<P3, P5<P4 and P6<P5.You will need to hold on this stock for a while. There is a possibility of small profits. Wait! There is also the probability of receiving additional benefits from this stock, like dividends, stock-splits, buyouts…...., if you hold on to your position.

2. **TIP:**Invest in fundamentally strong companies or companies which have undergone consolidation.

ACTION 12: P6>P5>P4>P3<P2<P1<P0

Date	Price	Action	Pattern
End Date D6	P6	P6>P5	+
D5	P5	P5>P4	+
D4	P4	P4>P3	+
D3	P3	P3<P2	-
D2	P2	P2<P1	-
D1	P1	P1<P0	-
Start Date D0	P0		

The I Ching Says:

1.The last three periods are on the upswing. If your stock is showing a definitive trend then take a position for a short period. This stock might exhibit sudden price reversal.

2. Hey! There is a probability of receiving additional benefits from this stock like dividends, stock-splits, buyouts…..., if you hold on to your position for the long term.

3. TIP: Investing/ trading in stocks of companies favored by analysts and institutional investors will be profitable.

ACTION 13: P6>P5>P4>P3>P2<P1>P0

Date	Price	Action	Pattern
End Date D6	P6	P6>P5	+
D5	P5	P5>P4	+
D4	P4	P4>P3	+
D3	P3	P3>P2	+
D2	P2	P2<P1	-
D1	P1	P1>P0	+
Start Date D0	P0		

The I Ching Says:

1.Expect a probable loss for this trade. There could be a price reversal after P6.

2. OR- You will need to hold on to this stock for a while if you bought during the above period.After initial setback, the price of your stock will recover.

3. TIP: Choose a stock which is the current market favorite.

ACTION 14: P6>P5<P4>P3>P2>P1>P0

Date	Price	Action	Pattern
End Date D6	P6	P6>P5	+
D5	P5	P5<P4	-
D4	P4	P4>P3	+
D3	P3	P3>P2	+
D2	P2	P2>P1	+
D1	P1	P1>P0	+
Start Date D0	P0		

The I Ching Says:

1.There are five pluses and one minus. P6>P5. If you plan your entry/exit points,you will do well in this trade. Use stop loss.

2.Beware! There is a possibility of price reversal.

3. TIP: Don't trade in institutional stocks.

ACTION 15: P6<P5<P4<P3>P2<P1<P0

Date	Price	Action	Pattern
End Date D6	P6	P6<P5	-
D5	P5	P5<P4	-
D4	P4	P4<P3	-
D3	P3	P3>P2	+
D2	P2	P2<P1	-
D1	P1	P1<P0	-
Start Date D0	P0		

The I Ching Says:

If the company's fundamentals are good, buy into this stock when the price is weak. Have a stop loss.Be patient and you will do very well in this trade.

ACTION 16: P6<P5<P4>P3<P2<P1<P0

Date	Price	Action	Pattern
End Date D6	P6	P6<P5	-
D5	P5	P5<P4	-
D4	P4	P4>P3	+
D3	P3	P3<P2	-
D2	P2	P2<P1	-
D1	P1	P1<P0	-
Start Date D0	P0		

The I Ching Says:

1.Plan your entry/exit points for this trade. Use stop loss. There could be a price reversal.

2.After initial setback, the price of your stock will recover.

ACTION 17: P6<P5>P4>P3<P2<P1>P0

Date	Price	Action	Pattern
End Date D6	P6	P6<P5	-
D5	P5	P5>P4	+
D4	P4	P4>P3	+
D3	P3	P3<P2	-
D2	P2	P2<P1	-
D1	P1	P1>P0	+
Start Date D0	P0		

The I Ching Says:

1.Choose a better stock than this one.

2. If you let your emotions influence this trade, expect a probable loss.

3. TIP: Choose a stock which is the current market favorite.

ACTION 18: P6>P5<P4<P3>P2>P1<P0

Date	Price	Action	Pattern
End Date D6	P6	P6>P5	+
D5	P5	P5<P4	-
D4	P4	P4<P3	-
D3	P3	P3>P2	+
D2	P2	P2>P1	+
D1	P1	P1<P0	-
Start Date D0	P0		

The I Ching Says:

1.Stay away, if the price of this stock is falling (P7<P6), thinly traded, or the company is facing management problems. Ask your broker about this company.

2. TIP: Don't trade in public sector stocks or stocks which depend upon government contracts.There are profit possibilities in stocks of companies which have restructured or made changes in its top management.

ACTION 19: P6<P5<P4<P3<P2>P1>P0

Date	Price	Action	Pattern
End Date D6	P6	P6<P5	-
D5	P5	P5<P4	-
D4	P4	P4<P3	-
D3	P3	P3<P2	-
D2	P2	P2>P1	+
D1	P1	P1>P0	+
Start Date D0	P0		

The I Ching Says:

1.This stock might exhibit sudden price swings. Buy on weakness and sell on strengths. Plan your entry/exit points, use stop loss and you will do well in this trade.

2. If you don't follow the above guidelines, expect a probable loss from this trade.

ACTION 20: P6>P5>P4<P3<P2<P1<P0

Date	Price	Action	Pattern
End Date D6	P6	P6>P5	+
D5	P5	P5>P4	+
D4	P4	P4<P3	-
D3	P3	P3<P2	-
D2	P2	P2<P1	-
D1	P1	P1<P0	-
Start Date D0	P0		

The I Ching Says:

1.This stock is showing an upswing. P5>P4 and P6>P5. Plan your entry/exit points for this trade. Use stop loss.Profits, if any, will not be much.

2.Expect a probable loss if you let your emotions influence this trade.

3. TIP: Choose a market favorite stock for short term trade.

ACTION 21: P6>P5<P4>P3<P2<P1>P0

Date	Price	Action	Pattern
End Date D6	P6	P6>P5	+
D5	P5	P5<P4	-
D4	P4	P4>P3	+
D3	P3	P3<P2	-
D2	P2	P2<P1	-
D1	P1	P1>P0	+
Start Date D0	P0		

The I Ching Says:

1. The whipsaw price movements suggest this stock is probably played by high frequency traders. If you take a position, expect a probable loss for this trade.

2. If you have jumped in, wait till the volatility subsides. The price of your stock will recover in due course.

3. TIP: Stay away, if this stock is thinly traded.Choose a better stock than this one.

ACTION 22: P6>P5<P4<P3>P2<P1>P0

Date	Price	Action	Pattern
End Date D6	P6	P6>P5	+
D5	P5	P5<P4	-
D4	P4	P4<P3	-
D3	P3	P3>P2	+
D2	P2	P2<P1	-
D1	P1	P1>P0	+
Start Date D0	P0		

The I Ching Says:

1.If this stock is an impulsive pick, watch out for price reversals.

2. If you have taken a position, wait. After initial setback, the price of your stock will recover.

3.Trust your judgment. Don't follow others advice.

ACTION 23: P6>P5<P4<P3<P2<P1<P0

Date	Price	Action	Pattern
End Date D6	P6	P6>P5	+
D5	P5	P5<P4	-
D4	P4	P4<P3	-
D3	P3	P3<P2	-
D2	P2	P2<P1	-
D1	P1	P1<P0	-
Start Date D0	P0		

The I Ching Says:

P6>P5. There are more minuses than pluses. Check out P7 to figure out the next price move. Expect mixed results with this stock.

ACTION 24: P6<P5<P4<P3<P2<P1>P0

Date	Price	Action	Pattern
End Date D6	P6	P6<P5	-
D5	P5	P5<P4	-
D4	P4	P4<P3	-
D3	P3	P3<P2	-
D2	P2	P2<P1	-
D1	P1	P1>P0	+
Start Date D0	P0		

The I Ching Says:

1. The downslide could continue. This stock will have few takers when you want to exit.Expect a probable loss for this trade.

2.If you have jumped in, expect see-saw price action for some time.You will need to wait till the price turns your way. Exit as soon as your trade is profitable.

ACTION 25: P6>P5>P4>P3<P2<P1>P0

Date	Price	Action	Pattern
End Date D6	P6	P6>P5	+
D5	P5	P5>P4	+
D4	P4	P4>P3	+
D3	P3	P3<P2	-
D2	P2	P2<P1	-
D1	P1	P1>P0	+
Start Date D0	P0		

The I Ching Says:

1.The price upswing is not sustainable. There is a probability of a sudden price reversal after you take a position in this stock.Exit as soon as your trade is profitable.

2. TIP: You will do well if you choose a better stock than this one.

ACTION 26: P6>P5<P4<P3>P2>P1>P0

Date	Price	Action	Pattern
End Date D6	P6	P6>P5	+
D5	P5	P5<P4	-
D4	P4	P4<P3	-
D3	P3	P3>P2	+
D2	P2	P2>P1	+
D1	P1	P1>P0	+
Start Date D0	P0		

The I Ching Says:

1.Successful trade if you set a target price to exit.

2.**OR**-Stay away, if this stock is thinly traded orexit from any open position ifP7 shows weakness.

ACTION 27: P6>P5<P4<P3<P2<P1>P0

Date	Price	Action	Pattern
End Date D6	P6	P6>P5	+
D5	P5	P5<P4	-
D4	P4	P4<P3	-
D3	P3	P3<P2	-
D2	P2	P2<P1	-
D1	P1	P1>P0	+
Start Date D0	P0		

The I Ching Says:

1.Expect mixed results with this stock.You will need to hold on to this stock for a while.

2.TIP: Trade in high probability stocks. Don't try a new/ unfamiliar trading strategy or invest/ trade in unknown stocks.

ACTION 28: P6<P5>P4>P3>P2>P1<P0

Date	Price	Action	Pattern
End Date D6	P6	P6<P5	-
D5	P5	P5>P4	+
D4	P4	P4>P3	+
D3	P3	P3>P2	+
D2	P2	P2>P1	+
D1	P1	P1<P0	-
Start Date D0	P0		

The I Ching Says:

1. If you have this stock, exit if you are showing a profit.However, this stock might have few takers when you want to exit.

2. If you take a position now, expect a probable loss for this trade.

3. TIP: Don't trade if your stock is a merger/ acquisition play or downgraded by analysts. Take a position in the stock of a company which has recently acquired a new promising company. Your profit probabilities are higher with stocks showing steadier price action than this stock.

ACTION 29: P6<P5>P4<P3<P2>P1<P0

Date	Price	Action	Pattern
End Date D6	P6	P6<P5	-
D5	P5	P5>P4	+
D4	P4	P4<P3	-
D3	P3	P3<P2	-
D2	P2	P2>P1	+
D1	P1	P1<P0	-
Start Date D0	P0		

The I Ching Says:

1.Wait for the market to stabilize before taking a position.

2.Don't expect much from this stock. You will need to hold on this stock for a while.

3.Expect a probable loss for this trade.

ACTION 30: P6>P5<P4>P3>P2< P1>P0

Date	Price	Action	Pattern
End Date D6	P6	P6>P5	+
D5	P5	P5<P4	-
D4	P4	P4>P3	+
D3	P3	P3>P2	+
D2	P2	P2<P1	-
D1	P1	P1<P0	-
Start Date D0	P0		

The I Ching Says:

1.Wait. The market's in a consolidation phase.

2.Limit your position in this stock. You will need to exit quickly to make a profit.

3. **TIP:**Trade in index stocks or stocks favored by institutions.

ACTION 31: P6<P5>P4>P3>P2<P1<P0

Date	Price	Action	Pattern
End Date D6	P6	P6<P5	-
D5	P5	P5>P4	+
D4	P4	P4>P3	+
D3	P3	P3>P2	+
D2	P2	P2<P1	-
D1	P1	P1<P0	-
Start Date D0	P0		

The I Ching Says:

1.Expect mixed results with this stock.

2.Wait for volatile conditions to subside before taking a position.

3.**TIP:** Wait for a better opportunity to present itself soon.

ACTION 32: P6<P5<P4>P3>P2>P1<P0

Date	Price	Action	Pattern
End Date D6	P6	P6<P5	-
D5	P5	P5<P4	-
D4	P4	P4>P3	+
D3	P3	P3>P2	+
D2	P2	P2>P1	+
D1	P1	P1<P0	-
Start Date D0	P0		

The I Ching Says:

1.Wait for volatile conditions to subside before taking a position.

2.Don't over leverage your position in this stock. Limit your position.Don't try to force this trade. This stock will not deliver a quick profit.

3.TIP:Your profit probabilities are higher with stocks of mid-size companies.

ACTION 33: P6>P5>P4>P3>P2<P1<P0

Date	Price	Action	Pattern
End Date D6	P6	P6>P5	+
D5	P5	P5>P4	+
D4	P4	P4>P3	+
D3	P3	P3>P2	+
D2	P2	P2<P1	-
D1	P1	P1<P0	-
Start Date D0	P0		

The I Ching Says:

1.The prices are on the upswing from P3 to P6. Check out P7 before taking a position.

2.Expect mixed results with this stock. It will be trading in a narrow range.

ACTION 34: P6<P5<P4>P3>P2>P1>P0

Date	Price	Action	Pattern
End Date D6	P6	P6<P5	-
D5	P5	P5<P4	-
D4	P4	P4>P3	+
D3	P3	P3>P2	+
D2	P2	P2>P1	+
D1	P1	P1>P0	+
Start Date D0	P0		

The I Ching Says:

1.After initial setback, the price of your stock will recover. But, don't try to force this trade. This stock will not deliver a quick profit.

2. Expect mixed results.

ACTION 35: P6>P5<P4>P3<P2<P1<P0

Date	Price	Action	Pattern
End Date D6	P6	P6>P5	+
D5	P5	P5<P4	-
D4	P4	P4>P3	+
D3	P3	P3<P2	-
D2	P2	P2<P1	-
D1	P1	P1<P0	-
Start Date D0	P0		

The I Ching Says:

1.This stock is probably influenced by high frequency traders.

2.If you love this stock, jump in when it starts showing a definitive trend.Limit your position in this stock. Plan your entry/exit points for this trade. Use stop loss.Have patience and you will be successful.

3.TIP: A stock tip from a reliable source might prove more profitable than your chosen stock.

ACTION 36: P6<P5<P4<P3>P2<P1>P0

Date	Price	Action	Pattern
End Date D6	P6	P6<P5	-
D5	P5	P5<P4	-
D4	P4	P4<P3	-
D3	P3	P3>P2	+
D2	P2	P2<P1	-
D1	P1	P1>P0	+
Start Date D0	P0		

The I Ching Says:

1.This stock is exhibiting price exhaustion. Short sell?But, don't over leverage your position in this stock. Use proper money management.

2. If you have already jumped in,you will need to hold on this stock till it shows a definitive trend.

3. TIP: Choose a better stock than this one.

ACTION 37: P6>P5>P4<P3>P2<P1>P0

Date	Price	Action	Pattern
End Date D6	P6	P6>P5	+
D5	P5	P5>P4	+
D4	P4	P4<P3	-
D3	P3	P3>P2	+
D2	P2	P2<P1	-
D1	P1	P1>P0	+
Start Date D0	P0		

The I Ching Says:

1.Your profit probabilities are higher with leading conservative stocks.

2. TIP: Be wary if your stock has been downgraded by analysts or is subject of rumors.

ACTION 38: P6>P5<P4>P3<P2>P1>P0

Date	Price	Action	Pattern
End Date D6	P6	P6>P5	+
D5	P5	P5<P4	-
D4	P4	P4>P3	+
D3	P3	P3<P2	-
D2	P2	P2>P1	+
D1	P1	P1>P0	+
Start Date D0	P0		

The I Ching Says:

1.If your stock has been out of favor expect some favorable news soon. So, after initial setback, the price of your stock will recover.

2. Wait, if your stock is trading in a narrow range.

3.TIP: Stay away from overpriced/ unknown/ under-performing or thinly traded stocks.

ACTION 39: P6<P5>P4<P3>P2<P1<P0

Date	Price	Action	Pattern
End Date D6	P6	P6<P5	-
D5	P5	P5>P4	+
D4	P4	P4<P3	-
D3	P3	P3>P2	+
D2	P2	P2<P1	-
D1	P1	P1<P0	-
Start Date D0	P0		

The I Ching Says:

1.Ask the advice of your stock broker / advisor before you trade this stock.

2.Wait for volatile conditions to subside before taking a position. Otherwise, expect a probable loss for this trade.

3. **TIP:**Wait for a better opportunity to present itself soon.

ACTION 40: P6<P5<P4>P3<P2>P1<P0

Date	Price	Action	Pattern
End Date D6	P6	P6<P5	-
D5	P5	P5<P4	-
D4	P4	P4>P3	+
D3	P3	P3<P2	-
D2	P2	P2>P1	+
D1	P1	P1<P0	-
Start Date D0	P0		

The I Ching Says:

1.Has the stock been downgraded? Ask the advice of your stock broker / advisor before you trade this stock.

2.Buy on weakness and sell on strengths. Have a stop loss for this trade so that you will be stopped out if there is a price reversal.

3. TIP: Your profit probabilities are higher with recovery stocks.

ACTION 41: P6>P5<P4<P3<P2>P1>P0

Date	Price	Action	Pattern
End Date D6	P6	P6>P5	+
D5	P5	P5<P4	-
D4	P4	P4<P3	-
D3	P3	P3<P2	-
D2	P2	P2>P1	+
D1	P1	P1>P0	+
Start Date D0	P0		

The I Ching Says:

1. What's your judgment about this stock? Why did you choose this stock? Is the company's earnings report out? Have analysts upgraded this stock?

2.You will do well in this trade with proper money management and patience.Exit as soon as your trade is profitable.

3.TIP: Close your unprofitable positions, if any, before taking fresh positions in any stock.

ACTION 42: P6>P5>P4<P3<P2< P1>P0

Date	Price	Action	Pattern
End Date D6	P6	P6>P5	+
D5	P5	P5>P4	+
D4	P4	P4<P3	-
D3	P3	P3<P2	-
D2	P2	P2<P1	-
D1	P1	P1>P0	+
Start Date D0	P0		

The I Ching Says:

1.This stock is played by high frequency traders.

2.Study the price charts. If your stock is showing a definitive trend then take a position.You will do well in this trade.

ACTION 43: P6<P5>P4>P3>P2>P1>P0

Date	Price	Action	Pattern
End Date D6	P6	P6<P5	-
D5	P5	P5>P4	+
D4	P4	P4>P3	+
D3	P3	P3>P2	+
D2	P2	P2>P1	+
D1	P1	P1>P0	+
Start Date D0	P0		

The I Ching Says:

1. Is P6 the beginning of the downswing?

2. Is there any unfavorable news about this company or the economy? Is the market turning bearish?

3.Expect mixed results with this stock.Set buy/ sell targets. Exit as soon as your trade is profitable.

ACTION 44: P6>P5>P4>P3>P2>P1<P0

Date	Price	Action	Pattern
End Date D6	P6	P6>P5	+
D5	P5	P5>P4	+
D4	P4	P4>P3	+
D3	P3	P3>P2	+
D2	P2	P2>P1	+
D1	P1	P1<P0	-
Start Date D0	P0		

The I Ching Says:

1.The entry price (P6) which you have planned for this stock is probably high.This stock will soon reach price exhaustion and start falling.

2.This stock will be whipsawed by high frequency trading. You will find it difficult to take profitable positions.

3. If you have jumped in, exit as soon as your position is profitable.

4. TIP: Your profit probabilities are higher with undervalued stocks.

ACTION 45: P6<P5>P4>P3<P2<P1<P0

Date	Price	Action	Pattern
End Date D6	P6	P6<P5	-
D5	P5	P5>P4	+
D4	P4	P4>P3	+
D3	P3	P3<P2	-
D2	P2	P2<P1	-
D1	P1	P1<P0	-
Start Date D0	P0		

The I Ching Says:

1.Limit your position in this stock. You will find it difficult to exit your position due to the stock's volatility.

2.Trade up after the price actionis on the upswing.

3. **TIP:**Choose a better stock than this one.Your profit probabilities are higher with leading stocks/ market favorites.

ACTION 46: P6<P5<P4<P3>P2>P1<P0

Date	Price	Action	Pattern
End Date D6	P6	P6<P5	-
D5	P5	P5<P4	-
D4	P4	P4<P3	-
D3	P3	P3>P2	+
D2	P2	P2>P1	+
D1	P1	P1<P0	-
Start Date D0	P0		

The I Ching Says:

1.Expect mixed results with this stock. Limit your initial position in this stock. Trade up after watching the price action.

2.TIP: Your profit probabilities are higher with leading stocks.

ACTION 47: P6<P5>P4>P3<P2>P1<P0

Date	Price	Action	Pattern
End Date D6	P6	P6<P5	-
D5	P5	P5>P4	+
D4	P4	P4>P3	+
D3	P3	P3<P2	-
D2	P2	P2>P1	+
D1	P1	P1<P0	-
Start Date D0	P0		

The I Ching Says:

1. If you have taken a position, you will need to hold on this stock for a while.Is the stock on the downswing? Also, this stock may have few takers for your exit price.

2.Wait, if the market appears to be in an over-bought situation.

3. TIP: Choose a better stock than this one.

ACTION 48: P6<P5>P4<P3>P2>P1<P0

Date	Price	Action	Pattern
End Date D6	P6	P6<P5	-
D5	P5	P5>P4	+
D4	P4	P4<P3	-
D3	P3	P3>P2	+
D2	P2	P2>P1	+
D1	P1	P1<P0	-
Start Date D0	P0		

The I Ching Says:

1.Choose a better stock than this one.

2.Your profit probabilities are higher with turnaround/ restructured stocks.

3.Stay away from falling/ unknown/ under-performing or thinly traded stocks.

ACTION 49: P6<P5>P4>P3>P2<P1>P0

Date	Price	Action	Pattern
End Date D6	P6	P6<P5	-
D5	P5	P5>P4	+
D4	P4	P4>P3	+
D3	P3	P3>P2	+
D2	P2	P2<P1	-
D1	P1	P1>P0	+
Start Date D0	P0		

The I Ching Says:

1.P6<P5. Wait for present conditions/ trend to change before taking a position.Study the price charts. If your stock is showing a definitive trend then take a position.

2. TIP: Trade in stocks of companies which have made changes in their top management.

79

ACTION 50: P6>P5<P4>P3>P2>P1<P0

Date	Price	Action	Pattern
End Date D6	P6	P6>P5	+
D5	P5	P5<P4	-
D4	P4	P4>P3	+
D3	P3	P3>P2	+
D2	P2	P2>P1	+
D1	P1	P1<P0	-
Start Date D0	P0		

The I Ching Says:

Choose your entry/exit points and you will make a profit.

ACTION 51: P6<P5<P4>P3<P2< P1>P0

Date	Price	Action	Pattern
End Date D6	P6	P6<P5	-
D5	P5	P5<P4	-
D4	P4	P4>P3	+
D3	P3	P3<P2	-
D2	P2	P2<P1	-
D1	P1	P1>P0	+
Start Date D0	P0		

The I Ching Says:

1. If you have taken a position, the price of your stock will recover after seven days.

2. If your stock's trend is not discernible at the moment, wait for present conditions/ trend to change before taking a position.

3. TIP: Choose another stock.

ACTION 52: P6>P5<P4<P3>P2<P1<P0

Date	Price	Action	Pattern
End Date D6	P6	P6>P5	+
D5	P5	P5<P4	-
D4	P4	P4<P3	-
D3	P3	P3>P2	+
D2	P2	P2<P1	-
D1	P1	P1<P0	-
Start Date D0	P0		

The I Ching Says:

1.The stock is in a volatile phase. Whipsaw price action.

2. If you have taken a position, you will need to hold on this stock for a while.

ACTION 53: P6>P5>P4<P3>P2<P1<P0

Date	Price	Action	Pattern
End Date D6	P6	P6>P5	+
D5	P5	P5>P4	+
D4	P4	P4<P3	-
D3	P3	P3>P2	+
D2	P2	P2<P1	-
D1	P1	P1<P0	-
Start Date D0	P0		

The I Ching Says:

1.Expect mixed results with this stock.

2.TIP: Stay away from volatile stocks or stocks of newer companies.

ACTION 54: P6<P5<P4>P3<P2>P1>P0

Date	Price	Action	Pattern
End Date D6	P6	P6<P5	-
D5	P5	P5<P4	-
D4	P4	P4>P3	+
D3	P3	P3<P2	-
D2	P2	P2>P1	+
D1	P1	P1>P0	+
Start Date D0	P0		

The I Ching Says:

1.Wait for the downslide to stop.

2. Study the price charts. If your stock is showing a definitive trend then take a position.

3. TIP: Wait for a better opportunity to present itself.

ACTION 55: P6<P5<P4>P3>P2<P1>P0

Date	Price	Action	Pattern
End Date D6	P6	P6<P5	-
D5	P5	P5<P4	-
D4	P4	P4>P3	+
D3	P3	P3>P2	+
D2	P2	P2<P1	-
D1	P1	P1>P0	+
Start Date D0	P0		

The I Ching Says:

1.Expect mixed results for this trade.

2. If you have jumped in, exit within ten days of taking a position.

3.TIP:Trade in trending stocks favored by analysts and institutional investors.

ACTION 56: P6>P5<P4>P3>P2<P1< P0

Date	Price	Action	Pattern
End Date D6	P6	P6>P5	+
D5	P5	P5<P4	-
D4	P4	P4>P3	+
D3	P3	P3>P2	+
D2	P2	P2<P1	-
D1	P1	P1<P0	-
Start Date D0	P0		

The I Ching Says:

1.There might be a slip up while conveying your order to your broker or the broker misinterpreting your instructions for this trade.Please ask your broker to strictly follow your instructions for this trade.

2.Profits, if any, will not be as per your expectation.

3.Expect a probable loss for this trade.

ACTION 57: P6>P5>P4<P3>P2>P1<P0

Date	Price	Action	Pattern
End Date D6	P6	P6>P5	+
D5	P5	P5>P4	+
D4	P4	P4<P3	-
D3	P3	P3>P2	+
D2	P2	P2>P1	+
D1	P1	P1<P0	-
Start Date D0	P0		

The I Ching Says:

1.Study the price chart. If your stock is showing a definitive trend then take a position. Stay with the trend.Don't over leverage your position in this stock. Limit your position.

2.This stock will be in the setback stage for three days and then recover for three days.

3.TIP: Don't trade on tips and rumors.

ACTION 58: P6<P5>P4>P3<P2>P1>P0

Date	Price	Action	Pattern
End Date D6	P6	P6<P5	-
D5	P5	P5>P4	+
D4	P4	P4>P3	+
D3	P3	P3<P2	-
D2	P2	P2>P1	+
D1	P1	P1>P0	+
Start Date D0	P0		

The I Ching Says:

1.Expect mixed results with this stock.The price of this stock might decline soon.Don't plan a fixed exit point for this stock. Exit as soon as your trade is profitable.

2. Check out the possibility of receiving additional benefits from this stock like dividends, stock-splits, buyouts.Ask our broker/ advisor.

ACTION 59: P6>P5>P4<P3<P2>P1<P0

Date	Price	Action	Pattern
End Date D6	P6	P6>P5	+
D5	P5	P5>P4	+
D4	P4	P4<P3	-
D3	P3	P3<P2	-
D2	P2	P2>P1	+
D1	P1	P1<P0	-
Start Date D0	P0		

The I Ching Says:

1.You will be fooled by false triggers for this stock. Plan your entry/exit points for this trade. Use stop loss.Profits, if any, will not be as per your expectation.

2.Is there a possibility of receiving additional benefits from this stock like dividends, stock-splits, buyouts? Ask your broker/ advisor.

3. TIP: Follow the herd.Your profit probabilities are higher with high volume stocks.

ACTION 60: P6<P5>P4<P3<P2>P1>P0

Date	Price	Action	Pattern
End Date D6	P6	P6<P5	-
D5	P5	P5>P4	+
D4	P4	P4<P3	-
D3	P3	P3<P2	-
D2	P2	P2>P1	+
D1	P1	P1>P0	+
Start Date D0	P0		

The I Ching Says:

1. Study the price chart. If your stock is showing a definitive trend then take a position.

2. If you have taken a position, after initial setback, the price of your stock will recover.

3.TIP: Choose familiar stocks. Stay away from unknown/ thinly traded or unfamiliar stocks.

ACTION 61: P6>P5>P4<P3<P2>P1>P0

Date	Price	Action	Pattern
End Date D6	P6	P6>P5	+
D5	P5	P5>P4	+
D4	P4	P4<P3	-
D3	P3	P3<P2	-
D2	P2	P2>P1	+
D1	P1	P1>P0	+
Start Date D0	P0		

The I Ching Says:

Trust your judgment on this stock. Expect mixed results. Choose your entry/exit prices and your trade will be profitable. Use stop loss.

ACTION 62: P6<P5<P4>P3>P2<P1<P0

Date	Price	Action	Pattern
End Date D6	P6	P6<P5	-
D5	P5	P5<P4	-
D4	P4	P4>P3	+
D3	P3	P3>P2	+
D2	P2	P2<P1	-
D1	P1	P1<P0	-
Start Date D0	P0		

The I Ching Says:

1.Your stock is not attractive at this price. You might have missed an opportunity, earlier.

2. If you still feel like jumping in, wait for volatile conditions to subside before taking a position. Plan your entry/exit points for this trade. Use stop loss.

ACTION 63: P6<P5>P4<P3>P2<P1>P0

Date	Price	Action	Pattern
End Date D6	P6	P6<P5	-
D5	P5	P5>P4	+
D4	P4	P4<P3	-
D3	P3	P3>P2	+
D2	P2	P2<P1	-
D1	P1	P1>P0	+
Start Date D0	P0		

The I Ching Says:

1.Today's trade could turn profitable in a week's time.After a severe initial setback, the price of your stock will recover.

2.You might be stopped out or you will exit in panic. Be patient. Have a contingency plan.

3. **TIP:**Stocks of companies situated in the West will do well.

ACTION 64: P6>P5<P4>P3<P2>P1<P0

Date	Price	Action	Pattern
End Date D6	P6	P6>P5	+
D5	P5	P5<P4	-
D4	P4	P4>P3	+
D3	P3	P3<P2	-
D2	P2	P2>P1	+
D1	P1	P1<P0	-
Start Date D0	P0		

The I Ching Says:

1.Limit your position. Exit as soon as your trade turns profitable.

2. TIP: Your profit probabilities are higher with overseas stocks.

THANK YOU!

Thank you for reading my book. If you enjoyed it, it would be greatly appreciated if you left a review so others can receive the same benefits you have. Your review will help me see what is and isn't working so I can better serve you and all my other readers even more.

https://www.amazon.com/dp/B01FM30HWK

http://ASIN.cc/2QV4XQL

Please visit my Amazon Author Page-

http://Author.to/MikeNach

Thanks again for your support!

MY OTHER BOOKS!

If you liked this book, you will like these too:

Investing:

I CHING OF THE STOCK MARKET

http://ASIN.cc/bxxqcL

https://www.createspace.com /5069717

THE 40 PARABLES OF INVESTING

http://ASIN.cc/11ujpiL

https://www.createspace.com /5029013

30 Essential Rules for New Investors

http://www.amazon.com/dp/B00ZS8ABUS

http://ASIN.cc/1fANORf

Christianity:

The Secret Gospel of Thomas: Decoded

http://www.amazon.com/dp/B00WX5FKE6

http://ASIN.cc/1Y9SQ8W

https://www.createspace.com/5470783

How to Be Enriched in Every Way

http://www.amazon.com/dp/B00M9CRXUW

http://ASIN.cc/12Jo4zL

https://www.createspace.com /5065824

Betrayer or the Chosen One? Judas Tells His Side

http://www.amazon.com/dp/B00XGFI1OS

http://ASIN.cc/1ZePUvf

I Have Sinned: The Judas Chronicles

http://ASIN.cc/26P4oxf

Eastern Religions:

Game of Illusions: Ashtavakra Gita

http://ASIN.cc/ytWryA

https://www.createspace.com /5042255

Game of Life: New Age Bhagavad Gita

http://ASIN.cc/1Q7_D9W

https://www.createspace.com/5344252

The Final Teachings of Lord Krishna: Uddhava Gita

http://www.amazon.com/dp/B0110B9ZWG

http://ASIN.cc/1ib2Sqf

Occult and Magick:

HOW TO BE THE MASTER OF THE UNIVERSE

http://ASIN.cc/ychKfq

https://www.createspace.com /5034839

HOW TO GET ANYTHING YOU WANT? MAKE A MAGICK MIRROR!

http://ASIN.cc/RahVJf

https://www.createspace.com/5040665

Fiction:

WHY ME? Abridged Version

http://ASIN.cc/e5qS5f

WHY ME? The Complete and Uncut Edition

http://www.amazon.com/dp/B017V5YI6S

http://ASIN.cc/22nkGcf

https://www.createspace.com/5860666

Advice:

THE HARE AND THE TORTOISE -BEAT THE BULLIES!

http://ASIN.cc/mocBz0

The Little Book That Beats the Bullies

http://ASIN.cc/12QD6kW

https://www.createspace.com /5043967

DATING ADVICE: 30 Frequently Asked Questions

http://ASIN.cc/V_YBvf

Notes

www.ingramcontent.com/pod-product-compliance
Lightning Source LLC
Chambersburg PA
CBHW070325190526
45169CB00005B/1755